essential DIY
projects

Mike Edwards/DIY Doctor

Hodder Education
338 Euston Road, London NW1 3BH.

Hodder Education is an Hachette UK company

First published in UK 2011 by Hodder Education.

This edition published 2011.

Copyright © Mike Edwards/DIY Doctor

The moral rights of the author have been asserted.
Database right Hodder Education (makers).

British Library Cataloguing in Publication Data: a catalogue record for this title is available from the British Library.

10 9 8 7 6 5 4 3 2 1

The publisher has used its best endeavours to ensure that any website addresses referred to in this book are correct and active at the time of going to press. However, the publisher and the author have no responsibility for the websites and can make no guarantee that a site will remain live or that the content will remain relevant, decent or appropriate.

The publisher has made every effort to mark as such all words which it believes to be trademarks. The publisher should also like to make it clear that the presence of a word in the book, whether marked or unmarked, in no way affects its legal status as a trademark.

Every reasonable effort has been made by the publisher to trace the copyright holders of material in this book. Any errors or omissions should be notified in writing to the publisher, who will endeavour to rectify the situation for any reprints and future editions.

Hachette UK's policy is to use papers that are natural, renewable and recyclable products and made from wood grown in sustainable forests. The logging and manufacturing processes are expected to conform to the environmental regulations of the country of origin.

www.hoddereducation.co.uk

Typeset by MPS Limited, a Macmillan Company.
Printed in Great Britain by CPI Cox & Wyman, Reading.

Contents

1

decorating

Most homeowners will want to decorate walls or ceilings at some time. These surfaces will probably have taken some knocks from normal living and will need to be filled in to avoid a bad finish. Although filling holes and dents is one of the most basic DIY tasks, it still requires practice. Practising using filler on the wall long before decoration is a good idea. New plaster must always be allowed to dry properly and sealed before decoration. This can take up to six weeks. When tiling or wallpapering, make sure you allow enough additional material for wastage. More time spent preparing the job properly will result in a much better finish.

1.1 Preparing new plaster for painting or papering

Painting

New plaster and new Artex are very porous indeed. If you apply any kind of ordinary paint directly onto either of these surfaces, moisture will immediately be sucked out of the paint, which will dry too quickly and will not stick properly. The paint may soon start to blister and flake off.

1 In a normal centrally heated house, allow four weeks for the plaster to dry before painting.

2 Prime or seal the surface first, i.e. apply a coating which is diluted enough to enter the pores of the material with the emulsion or liquid with which it is mixed. So, if you intend to use water-based paint, e.g. emulsion, then mix some of that emulsion paint with water at a ratio of 4 parts paint to 1 part water and stir thoroughly.

3 Apply this to the surface – you might actually hear the plaster or Artex sucking up the liquid. It is rarely necessary to apply two coats of sealer, but it will not harm the surface either.

4 When the surface is sealed and dry, you can continue to paint as normal.

The humidity in kitchens and bathrooms allows water-based paints, like normal emulsion, to soak up the water vapour, which can make them unstable and likely to peel or harbour mould spores. To avoid these problems, it is advisable to use oil-based paint in kitchens and bathrooms. Some companies make special kitchen and bathroom paint in a great range of colours.

Mould prevention chemicals can be mixed with normal emulsions to prevent bathroom mould.

If you are in a real hurry to paint your wall, use microporous paint, which allows the surface of the plaster to carry on breathing and evaporating moisture while it is drying out. These paints should not be painted onto wet plaster – at least two weeks' drying time should be allowed in a normally heated house. The paints can be found in many DIY stores and decorators' merchants. They are generally a lot thinner than ordinary water- or solvent-based paints and in many cases, once the wall is dry, it is recommended that you paint over them with emulsion. Please read the instructions on the container for information regarding thinning down and applying the first coat onto new plaster.

Wallpapering

To hang wallpaper to new walls:

1 In a normal centrally heated house, allow four weeks for the plaster to dry before papering.
2 Once they are dry, 'size' the walls. Size is a proprietary product for sealing the walls but a dilution of the wallpaper paste you are going to use can also be used as a form of size to seal the wall. Most pastes give a sizing solution on the packet, but a rough guide is to use 25 per cent more water in a sizing solution.
3 Apply the size or diluted paste with a large emulsion brush.

1.2 Blocking stains before decoration

If you have a water stain on the ceiling or wall, the first thing to do is to make absolutely sure the leak or other source of water causing the stain has been dealt with. Disguising water leaks in any way will only lead to further problems, as the water will find its way into the room somewhere else. Once you are sure you have dealt with the source of the water you can undertake the following project.

If you have had a leak coming through a painted ceiling, or damp coming through an old wall, it does not matter how many coats of emulsion, or how many layers of wallpaper you put on, the stain will still come through. The only way to stop this happening is to cover the stain with a stain blocker, solvent or an oil-based paint first. You can then emulsion or paper on top of this.

You will need:

* sugar soap for fire damage, grease problems in the kitchen, soot or nicotine stains
* a stain blocker, solvent or an oil-based paint.

To cover the stain:

1 Ensure the cause of the stain has been dealt with.
2 In the event of fire damage, grease problems in the kitchen, soot or nicotine stains, the areas concerned must be washed down thoroughly with a solution of sugar soap. Sugar soap is a crystallized alkaline (which looks like sugar in its powdered form), which can be bought in DIY stores in powder or liquid forms.
3 Apply a stain blocker, solvent or an oil-based paint. The stain blockers you can buy in DIY stores are usually solvent-based and require a lot of ventilation when they are applied, so keep the windows open.
4 Once this has dried completely you can decorate over it as you choose, with emulsion or with wallpaper.

1.3 Ceramic tiling

Ceramic wall tiles are made in an enormous variety of colours, designs and sizes. You will need to spend some time looking at displays to find the tiles that appeal most to you. Keep an eye open for combination tiles. These are basically tiles with the same background colour as the majority being used but with decorated tiles in singles, or sets of two or three. These are used almost like pictures on a wall, being interspaced with the plain tiles. Many of these decorative tiles are hand-painted before being glazed and can bring a tiled wall to life. Look out also for tiles that are a colour match for modern sanitary ware.

Wall tiles sizes are most commonly 150 mm × 150 mm (6 inches × 6 inches), 200 mm × 200 mm (8 inches × 8 inches), 200 mm × 250 mm (8 inches × 10 inches) and 200 mm × 300 mm (8 inches × 12 inches). As a general rule, aim for large tiles in a large room and small tiles in a small room. This is partly for aesthetic reasons and partly for practical reasons. The larger the tile, the quicker it is to finish!

Working out wall tile quantities

1 The easiest method of working out how many tiles you need is to measure the height of the wall and calculate how many of your chosen tile size will be needed to fit from floor to ceiling.

2 Count any halves or parts of a tile as a whole one.

3 Do the same for the wall width.

4 Multiply the number required for the height by the number for the width and this will give you the total number of tiles needed for the wall.

5 Repeat the process for the other walls.

6 Use the same process to deduct for doors and windows where you will not be tiling, but do not forget the 'reveals' or window returns and any sills you intend to tile.

7 When you have a total for the whole room, add 10 per cent, i.e. add a further 10 tiles for every 100 that your calculations say you need. This is to allow for mistakes and breakages and to make sure you have some tiles of the same colour should any get broken later on.

Example: A wall 2.7 m long by 2.2 m high is to be tiled using 150 mm × 150 mm tiles. Divide the wall height by the tile height: 2,200 ÷ 150 = 14.67 (15 tiles). Then divide wall length by tile width: 2,700 ÷ 150 = 18. Tiles required are 15 × 18 = 270. Add 10 per cent (27) means you need to buy 297 tiles. Check the boxes for the number of tiles in each and get enough to match the number you need.

Adhesives and grout

* The long-term success of your tiling depends to a large extent on the adhesives you use to bond the tiles to the wall and you should always select the correct adhesive for any particular situation. For wall tiling work in bathrooms you need a water-resistant tile adhesive. Water-resistant adhesive is slightly more expensive than standard adhesive but do not be tempted to cut corners.

* All ceramic tile adhesives have full instructions printed on the containers and these should be followed to the letter.
* The spaces between the tiles are filled with a grouting compound and again, in a bathroom, this must be a water-resistant grout. The grout can be purchased already mixed or in powder form to mix by hand. It is very easy to mix.
* Adhesive and grout containers state the coverage on the containers, so check this out before buying.

Preparation

* Remove any and all wallpaper. The adhesion to the wall is only good if the tiles are actually fixed to the wall. Fixing to paper means that if the paper is not fixed well, or the tile adhesive dissolves the wallpaper paste, the whole lot could be on the floor by the time you go to bed.
* Old tiling does not necessarily have to be removed, but the complications involved in tiling over existing tiles make it rarely worth the effort.
* Clean down the walls with sugar soap to remove any grease.
* New plaster should be allowed to dry completely and then sealed with a mist coat of emulsion (2 parts emulsion to 1 part water). Absorbent surfaces can also be sealed with PVA building adhesive diluted 1 part adhesive to 5 parts water. Sealer must be completely dry before tiling is started.

Tiling

You will need:
* a spirit level or plumb bob
* a good-quality tile cutter, either hand operated or electrical (get the best you can afford as it makes the job so much easier)
* pincers, pliers or a tile saw
* tiles

* plastic spacers to keep a uniform gap that is wide enough (usually 2 mm) to allow you to force grout in
* a measuring gauge made from a piece of timber (18 mm × 44 mm wide and about 1.8 mm or 2.4 mm long) marked out in exact tile widths, including the spaces in between
* a timber batten the length of the wall to be tiled
* a pencil
* adhesive
* grout
* adhesive comb or notched trowel.

Timber marked out in tile widths and grout gaps

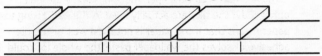

1 Open all the boxes of tiles and shuffle them around. This distributes any colour variations and makes them unnoticeable over the wall.
2 Determine a starting point for your tiling by fixing a perfectly straight length of timber horizontally to the wall, with the top edge just over one tile height above the highest floor or skirting board level.

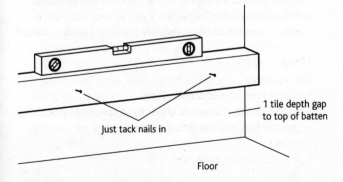

Just tack nails in

1 tile depth gap to top of batten

Floor

3 Use a spirit level to check that the batten is truly horizontal. This batten, going the full width of the wall, will provide the level at which tiling commences, and will ensure that tiling lines are straight even though the floor may be uneven. Don't drive the nails fully home – they have to be removed later.

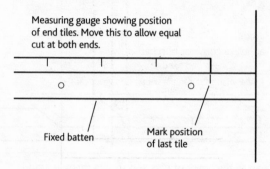

Measuring gauge showing position of end tiles. Move this to allow equal cut at both ends.

Fixed batten

Mark position of last tile

4 Use your measuring gauge vertically from the fixed batten to check that at the top of the wall you are not left with a narrow strip to be tiled. Narrow tile strips are difficult to cut.

5 If this situation arises, drop the horizontal fixed batten to leave roughly equal spacing at the top and bottom of the wall for cut tiles.

6 Measure to find the centre point of the fixed batten (the centre point along the width of the wall). Mark this point on the batten.

7 Use your measuring gauge horizontally along the batten to determine where the last whole tile will be fixed close to the end of the wall. Mark this point on the fixed batten.

8 Use a spirit level to fix a batten vertically up the wall, starting from your mark representing the end of the last full tile in the row.

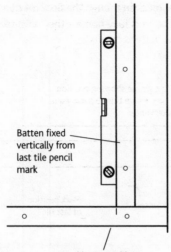

Batten fixed
vertically from
last tile pencil
mark

Fixed horizontal batten

9 When the vertical batten is fixed (remember, this too has to come off again, so don't fix it too well) lay six or eight tiles loose in the right-angled corner you have formed to make sure they sit straight. You should be able to see at a glance if the joints seem to be closing up, indicating that the two battens are not meeting at right angles to each other.

10 It is very rare that walls in a property are absolutely square with each other, so fix all of the full tiles first and then make any cuts into the abutting walls, floor or ceiling. Start tiling in the corner. Follow the instructions supplied with the adhesive, spreading an area of about 1 square metre at a time, then comb it out.

11 Place the tiles firmly onto the ribbed adhesive, with spacers set in between.

12 Working sideways and upwards, complete the fixing of all whole tiles, then leave for about 24 hours to dry.

13 Remove the battens carefully.

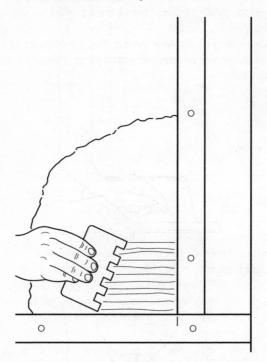

14 Cut tiles to fit around the perimeter. Where space is limited, the adhesive can be applied to the back of the cut tiles instead of onto the wall. The simplest method of cutting the wall tiles is to mark the glazed tile surface where it is to be cut then, with the help of a straight edge, score the surface with the tile cutter to break the glaze. Place the scored tile over a couple of matchsticks or spacers, then press down either side to snap the tile.

15 Pincers, pliers or a tile saw can be used to cut corners or curves out of tiles, to fit around projections. Again, the surface should be scored before the waste area is nibbled away.

16 When tiling is complete and has dried for 24 hours, all tile spacers should be removed and all joints filled well with grout.

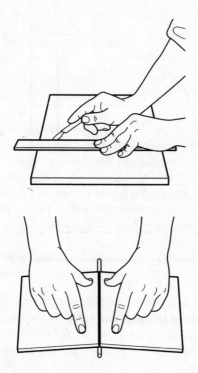

1.4 Wallpapering

Most wallpapers come is a standard size of 530 mm wide by 10.5 m long. Woodchip paper and lining paper, along with a few other 'specials' come in longer or differing width rolls. You can measure round the room for the number of rolls you need using the chart below.

Perimeter of room	Height of wall		
	2.3–2.4 m	2.4–2.6 m	2.6–2.7 m
10 m	5 rolls	5 rolls	6 rolls
12 m	6 rolls	6 rolls	7 rolls
14 m	7 rolls	7 rolls	8 rolls
16 m	8 rolls	8 rolls	9 rolls
18 m	9 rolls	9 rolls	10 rolls
20 m	10 rolls	10 rolls	11 rolls

Make sure all the rolls of paper you buy have the same batch number on them, and do not be tempted to try to 'stretch' the quantity you need. If there are windows and doors in the room, do not deduct rolls for them – there will be wastage and if you run out of paper it may be very hard to get one extra roll with exactly the same colour match. It is much better to buy one roll more than you need. You will always have some paper left over to patch up if necessary.

If you are going to use wallpaper in your home you will need the right tools. As usual, get the best tools you can afford.

You will need:
* wallpaper (the correct amount for your room – see the table above)
* a tape measure
* a pencil

* a spirit level
* paperhanging scissors
* a pasting table
* a paste bucket
* a pasting brush
* a paper-hanging brush
* a seam roller
* a sharp hobby knife or proprietary wallpaper trimming knife
* overlap adhesive if you are using washable or vinyl paper.

To hang your wallpaper:

1 Make sure the surface of your wall is free from flaking paint or grease and never paper over existing wallpaper. The paste on the new wallpaper can soak through to any existing wallpaper, dissolving it.

2 Check the pattern on the paper (the label will help here). Some papers have a random pattern so it does not matter where you join the lengths. Some have a pattern that only matches at specific distances; there may be a little more wastage with this type of match. Generally, even a staggered match is repeated within 100 mm.

3 Decide where you are going to start papering. If the room has a focal point, e.g. a fireplace, then begin there, especially with large-patterned paper, by centring the pattern over the focal point. If there is no obvious focal point, start at a corner, ideally on a wall where there are no windows or doors. Wallpaper round the room in a clockwise direction.

4 Mark a vertical plumb line on which to start your papering. (It is important to remember that the corners of your room are extremely unlikely to be absolutely vertical or square, so you need to make sure the very first strip of paper you put up is plumb.)

5 Then measure along the wall, from one corner of the room, the width of your wallpaper less 25 mm, and mark a vertical line from ceiling to skirting board, using a spirit level. This line is the leading edge of your paper and when the first strip is hung it will go round the corner by about 25 mm.

6 Measure the height of your room in a number of places. It will probably vary by a few millimetres.

7 Now cut some lengths of wallpaper to length, adding 100 mm (more if the pattern requires it) to the longest measurement to allow for trimming. Remember to allow for pattern repetitions.

8 Lay your lengths of paper face down on the pasting table. Prevent the ends from curling back up into a roll by tying a piece of string across the table to the legs.

9 Mix the paste in the bucket as per the instructions on the packet. Tie another piece of string across the paste bucket at the point where the handle joins the top of the bucket. This will give you something to rest the brush bristles on to avoid getting the handle covered in paste.

10 Paste the paper by working from the middle of each length to the outside. Fold the wet sides together as shown and move to one side to store. If you are careful and line up the lengths you have cut with the top edge of the table you should be able to paste three or four lengths before hanging them. Some papers need to soak for a while before hanging, so check the instructions on the label.

11 Take the first length and place the edge against the line on the wall. Unfold the paper gently onto the wall, using your hanging brush to brush down the middle and out towards both edges. This brushing makes sure that the paper makes contact with the wall and at the same time brushes out any air bubbles that may have been trapped under the paper.

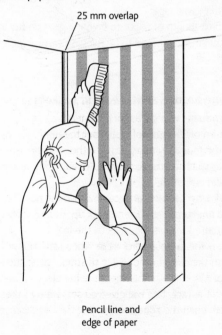

25 mm overlap

Pencil line and edge of paper

12 Brush the paper up to the crease between ceiling and wall and also the crease between skirting board and wall.

13 Double-check that the edge of the paper is in your pencil plumb line and then press the paper into both the creases with the back edge of your paperhanging scissors. This should give you a line to cut along.

14 Pull the paper off the wall far enough to cut it and then brush it back into place.

15 Brush the paper tightly into the corner of the room and you should have about 25 mm overlap on the adjoining wall. This can be trimmed back to about 5 mm or 10 mm – this will be covered later by another length of wallpaper.

16 The next length of paper to be hung goes on the line also, so you are guaranteed to be hanging vertical lengths around the room.

Cutting around switches and sockets

When you get to a switch or socket:

1 First, turn off the power supply to that unit.

2 Mark the four corners as shown in the diagram opposite and cut diagonally across to leave an opening slightly smaller than the faceplate of the socket or switch.

3 Cut off most of the four flaps as shown by the dotted line. Leave enough to tuck behind the socket or switch.

4 Unscrew the faceplate from the wall a little and wiggle it through the cut paper, pushing the paper against the wall as you do.

5 Tighten the faceplate back to the wall and turn the power back on when the adhesive is dry.

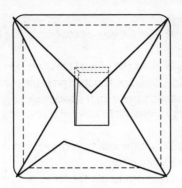

Papering around windows and door openings

1 Cut the first overlap on a window as shown by 1 in the following diagram.

2 Fold the flaps round into the window reveal, and smooth the rest of the paper above and below the window, cutting it out around the windowsill.

3 Next, cut and paste the two top lengths above the window (see 2 in the diagram), folding them down and under the head of the window opening.

4 Now cut and paste the two corresponding strips under the window.

5 Note that the cut widths may not work out evenly at either side of the window. Measure to see if the joint between the strips of paper marked 2 in the diagram comes close to the centre of the window. If it does not, then it is fine to start hanging paper at point 2, either side of the centre of the window, and work out in both directions to the corner of the room. This way you should avoid silly strips of paper running down the window frame.

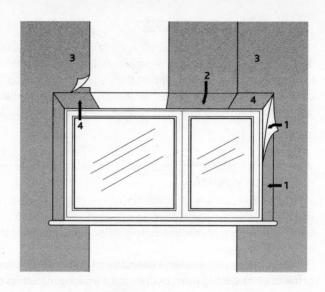

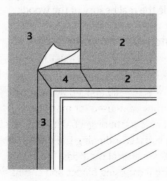

6 Now cut pieces of paper to fit under the head of the window opening (4 in the diagram). It is as well to cut and paste these pieces before finally pasting lengths 1 and 3. These pieces (4) can then be turned up onto the wall above the window where lengths 1 and 3 will cover them.

7 Hang strip 3 in the same way as you did strip 1.

Papering behind radiators

Wherever possible, take the radiator off the wall (after draining down the system if necessary). This makes for a much better job. If this is not possible, cut the paper to the required shape to drop down over the radiator brackets, then smooth it out using a radiator paint roller.

1.5 Stripping paint

Why strip paint?

Repainting a surface, especially timber, can only be done so many times before the paint starts to show signs of being tired. When this happens you really need to strip the paint off back to the wood and start again.

There are also times when a natural wood grain finish may look better than the existing paint, or when some amazing mouldings or furniture have been covered by a paint-happy person who simply wanted to hide the real beauty of the wood.

Stripping paint from timber

The three ways of stripping paint from timber are:
* using heat to lift the paint off the surface – nowadays the heat is usually applied by proprietary heat guns, but blowlamps were used for many years
* using liquid paste or gel paint stripper, either applying it to the surface or dipping the painted object into a vat of stripper (chemical methods)
* scraping it off using blades and chisels and then sanding it down, or just sanding it down (mechanical methods).

The chemicals used are extremely toxic and, as with all DIY work, you must take care to protect yourself and others. Masks, goggles and gloves should be worn with all stripping techniques. Chemical strippers can also affect the glue used in timber joints.

1.6 Painting timber

Any decoration job, either DIY or professionally done, is only ever as good as the preparation and thought that has gone into it. If, for example, you are going to varnish a surface, sanding the timber across the grain prior to varnishing will leave scratches, which will show through the varnish and ruin your work. As the painting itself is fairly straightforward, this project concentrates on the all-important preparation, followed by some top painting tips.

Basics

1 Clean the surface before painting it. There is grease in the air in every home, from cooking and general cleaning. This grease settles on all surfaces and must be removed. Paint, if it is to stay where it is put, must have a stable base.

2 For the best results, use the best brushes you can afford. Cheap brushes will not only lose bristles quickly but will leave brush marks much more easily in the paint.

3 Sand new or bare timber and then prime it before you paint it. Sandpaper is available with different degrees of coarseness of the surface. These are called grades. The grades are measured in numbers and the lower the number the coarser the grit. New timber should be sanded with medium to fine paper of about 120 grade. For large areas, an electrical sander may be ideal. Using rolls of abrasive paper makes it easy to cut to length to fit in most power sanders.

4 After sanding there may be little indents that need to be filled. Nail heads, etc. can spoil your paint finish. A very popular myth among DIY enthusiasts is that paint can fill holes. This is not true! All-purpose filler will usually do the trick or, for varnished surfaces, a wood filler should be used that matches the colour of the wood as closely as possible.

Priming the woodwork

Always apply a primer before painting. If an undercoat or topcoat of paint is applied to bare wood, the moisture is sucked out of it too quickly and the paint does not have a chance to soak into the timber. The paint therefore dries on the surface and will quickly peel. Primer is a thin paint that soaks into the grain slightly and takes some of the porosity out of the new or bare timber. The primer itself can only soak in properly if the surface is free from grease and the grain is a little open to receive it.

1 If necessary, wash down the woodwork with a solution of sugar soap which will degrease it.

2 Sand the surface with a medium grit sandpaper. The best sandpapers are aluminium oxide or silicone carbide papers, which are a little more expensive but stay workable longer.

3 It is always best to wrap the paper around a sanding block to keep a flat surface with which to sand. If the timber has different contours, such as chamfered architrave or skirting, wrapping the paper round a firm sponge will allow the paper to get into and onto the contours.

4 Apply the primer once the sanding is complete.

You do not need to remove all the paint on previously painted surfaces if it is not flaking and is in a stable condition. Simply clean thoroughly with sugar soap and then sand down with a fine paper to give a key for the new paint.

If the existing paint is not in good condition, it may be as well to remove it. This is usually easiest done using a paint stripper (see 1.5).

If only small areas of the paintwork need to be removed, sand them down as smoothly as possible, creating a very gentle slope between the existing paint and the wood underneath. Then spot prime the areas of new wood with primer and carry on painting with undercoat and gloss.

Wear a mask for sanding existing paintwork as older paints may contain lead which can be dangerous. The safest way is to use 'wet and dry' paper and keep it wet.

Undercoat

When the timber is sealed and primed it can be undercoated. The undercoat provides a film of paint that forms a non-absorbent, flexible base for the top, decorative coat. The undercoat, ideally, should be as close as possible to the colour of the chosen topcoat.

An undercoat is always a good idea on previously painted surfaces as it will give you a much better finish and stops the paint 'dragging' on the surface.

Painting tips and problem solving

* **Topcoat** The topcoat is usually a gloss, matt or eggshell paint that is suitable for the location of the work.

* **Top-quality gloss finish** To get a gloss finish that looks really good, wait for the first coat to dry completely, then use 600 grade 'wet and dry' paper with water over the surface. Wipe off the excess water with kitchen towel. The next coat will look almost like glass. Do this again for a third coat that will look like glass.

* **Sticky door** If you have just painted a door and are worried about it sticking, as they all do, wait for it to dry and rub the edges with a candle before closing.

* **Keep your cool** When painting the outside of your house, try to avoid dark colours. They absorb heat very easily and are much more prone to blistering as a result. Also try to paint the walls in the following order: west facing in the morning, east in the afternoon, and south and north when they are shaded the most. Painting in direct sunlight can make the paint dry in a patchy way and can give a poor finish.

* **Old paint** If you have half a tin of paint that you need to keep, turn it upside down before storing it (making sure the lid is fixed firmly!). This will remove the need for cutting away a skin when you use it again. If you have not done this and find you have bits in your paint, strain it through an old pair of tights before you use it.

* **Smelly paint** To get rid of the smell of fresh paint, cut an onion in half and leave it in the room. It will take away most of the smell.

* **Wall lights** Cover wall lights with a plastic carrier bag when decorating. It will save you hours of cleaning time.

* **Easy stripping** If you have any wallpaper to strip, go to the chemist and buy some alum. Fill a bucket with water and add two teaspoons of alum to each pint of water. Wet the paper thoroughly and allow it to dry in. It should then lift off the wall much more easily.

* **Masking alternative** Masking paper can be a pain to get off glass and can easily leave marks that are worse than the paint would have been. Spend some time cutting newspaper into strips and dampen each strip before using it as masking tape. The dampness will allow you to manoeuvre it into position and keep it stuck to the glass long enough for you to paint your frame. It falls off easily afterwards!

* **Roll it up** If you have finished with your emulsion roller and brush for the day, but intend to carry on tomorrow or in a few days' time, wrap them tightly in cling-film or a plastic bag. They will stay soft and usable for up to a month if wrapped properly.

* **Gloss over it** To have the same effect with your gloss brush, keep it in a jar full of water, or at least so that the water is over the bristles and retaining band. Shake it out the next day and carry on.

* **Paint thinners** Don't waste your thinners – cut the top from a plastic drinks bottle and use that for cleaning your brushes.

* **Old brushes** Hard brushes can be rejuvenated after a spell in hot vinegar. Comb the bristles with a fork afterwards and keep in shape with an elastic band until dry.

* **Old tins in the shed** Keep track of the paint you have saved by sticking a piece of masking tape down one side of the tin. When you have finished painting, mark a line on the tape to indicate the top of the paint, and it might be handy to write on the date as well. No more wrestling the top off to find you haven't got enough paint for the job.

* **Messy roller tray** Before you start painting, wrap your roller tray in cling-film and just roll it up and throw it away afterwards.

* **Painting chairs** Stand your chair legs in saucers or something similar to avoid ground contact or balancing acts!
* **Messy handles** Keep paint off door handles, hinges and locks by applying some Vaseline, on a piece of tissue, to them before you start painting. The paint won't stick to this.
* **Putty mess** If the putty you want to use is very oily and too soft, roll it around on a piece of newspaper first. This will soak up the excess oil and make it ready for use. Keep it soft by wrapping it in cling-film or silver foil.
* **Rejuvenating masking tape** Put the tape in a microwave oven with a glass of water. Set the oven on full for about 1 minute. Switch off and check that the tape has become quite warm (do not overheat). The tape will now peel off just as it did when new. When the tape becomes cold, just reactivate it.
* **Sticky tin** When you have opened and stirred a new tin of paint, tie a piece of string tightly between the two rivets where the handle connects. This will enable you to wipe your brush and rest it without getting paint all over yourself or the tin.

Faults in painted surfaces

Faults in painted surfaces are a nuisance and can sometimes be avoided. Here are some common faults.

* **Grey/white surface haze** Sometimes called 'blooming', this is a result of the paint being affected by moisture during drying. The moisture can be from condensation in an unventilated room or water from another source, such as rainfall.
* **Blistering** This is almost always caused by moisture in the timber, which has been painted over without being allowed to dry properly. The moisture tries to evaporate but cannot get through the paint. The paint will eventually crack and peel, allowing more moisture in. Windowsills are very prone

to these blisters, sometimes because the ends of the sills have not been prepared properly, allowing the moisture in. This fault often occurs on metal surfaces as well, due to the surface not being properly prepared before painting, including rust removal and the use of a primer. The interaction between two different metal surfaces can cause 'electrolytic corrosion', which may also lead to blistering.

* **Cracking** Sometimes called 'checking' or 'aligatoring', this usually happens in regular cracking patterns on the surface of the paint. This is caused by applying the top coat of paint before the one beneath it is completely dry – the coats will dry at different rates, causing shrinkage.

* **Peeling** If areas of paint can be easily peeled off it is most commonly due to a contaminated surface or the use of the wrong (or no) primer.

* **No shine to gloss** This will happen if the primer used is too thin or if insufficient primer or undercoat has been used. The absorbent timber will soak the paint in too quickly and leave a poor finish.

* **Slow drying** This is generally caused by moisture contamination, old paint whose drying agent has evaporated, or low temperatures.

* **Wrinkles** Too much paint applied in one go on a vertical surface will cause the paint to run, drying with a 'wrinkled' appearance.

2

plumbing

Blocked drains, a toilet that won't flush and dripping taps are some of the most common problems that occur in the house. Whilst large DIY jobs will need to be carried out by a qualified professional, there is no good reason to call out a plumber and pay for simple things such as fixing a dripping tap.

The projects in this chapter will show you that for many household plumbing jobs, the DIY solution is a perfectly viable option. Before you undertake any plumbing work it may be worthwhile drawing up a diagram of your water system. This will help you understand the plumbing in your house and make it easier to deal with problems when they occur.

2.1 Repairing a burst copper pipe

This method of repairing a copper pipe can also be used if you have accidentally punctured a pipe, for example with a nail.

You will need:

* a hacksaw
* some emery paper, glass paper or a file
* a slip coupler of the right size for the pipe
* an adjustable spanner or one of the right size to tighten the nuts on the coupler.

Proprietary slip couplers, available for all sizes of pipe, can be bought from plumbers' merchants and, ideally, all DIY enthusiasts will have one of these in their toolbox. It is a sheath with an internal diameter slightly larger than the copper pipe it will cover.

To mend the pipe:

1 First, turn off the water at the mains as soon as you realize there is a problem. A small amount of water will dry out reasonably quickly; a large amount of water can cause a great deal of damage. If you do not know where your mains stopcock is, go and find it now!

2 Locate the damaged area of the pipe. Remember, this may not be directly behind the visible signs of water. The ceiling may slope, or the pressure may have forced a spray of water away from the actual split, so search thoroughly.

3 The hole, burst or split in the pipe will only be small, so cut the pipe either side of it with a hacksaw. The saw will leave burrs around the edges of the cuts and these need to be smoothed off with some emery paper, glass paper or a file. (Even when the water is turned off and the system is drained down, there will be water in the pipes. As you cut, be prepared for this with some cloths and a small bowl.)

4 Undo the slip coupling into its various component parts. Take the nuts from each end, releasing the two olives, as shown in the diagram. The olives are brass rings that are squeezed between the fitting and the pipe by the action of tightening the end nuts up against them. This fills the joint

between slip coupling and pipe, preventing water seeping through.

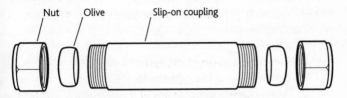

Nut   Olive   Slip-on coupling

5 Place a nut over each end of the cut pipe, then slide on the two olives. Then slide the slip coupling on to one of the cut ends of the pipe and push it back over the other end of the cut pipe. Position the slip coupling so that the cut-out section of the pipe is roughly in the middle, and then slide the two olives up to it. Then tighten the nuts at each end of the slip coupling.

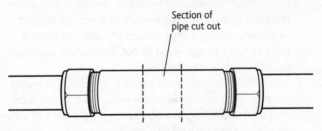

Section of
pipe cut out

Tighten both nuts ensuring
centering of slip-on coupling

6 Tightening should not be overdone and, if done carefully, you should be able to feel the olive squeezing closed. Overtightening will cause leaks as it can squash the copper pipe, so it is better to tighten to a point where you can feel good resistance on the nuts. If you have not tightened the fitting enough, you will only get a small drip when you turn the water on, which you can stop by tightening a little more. This is a tiny job compared with overtightening and having to start again.

7 Turn on the water and check that there are no leaks.

2.2 Repairing a dripping tap

The principles of tap operation are the same with most taps, and the illustration below can be referred to for the names of the various parts of a tap. Essentially, turning the handle of a tap turns a spindle, which in turn lifts a valve (called a jumper), together with a rubber washer, from the tap inlet. This allows water to flow through the spout.

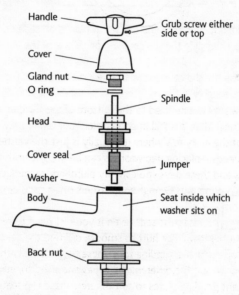

You will need:
* a good adjustable spanner or a plumber's wrench
* a grinding tool, usually called a tap reseating tool.

To repair the tap:
1 First, turn off the water and, if you are working on an upstairs tap, open one of the taps downstairs to drain the pipes.
2 Prise up the cover of the tap or remove the screw at the side of the handle to allow access to the gland nut which holds the spindle and jumper in place.

3 Once this nut is undone you will be able to lift out the tap mechanism to get to the seat.

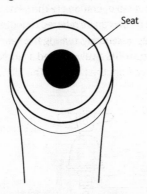

Seat

4 The washer will be fixed to the bottom of the jumper, so first check that it is still in good order. Your repair may well be one of the lucky few where it actually is just the washer that needs replacing. Tap washers can be bought from DIY stores and these days you can buy plumbers' repair kits that contain numerous O rings and washers often used around the home.

5 Once you can see the seat (even if you just need to replace the washer it will not hurt to smooth or grind the seat down a little), insert the grinding tool. These tools come with various threads to suit the different tap types and sizes, together with different grinding plates to suit different sized tap seats.

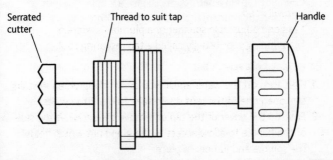

Serrated cutter

Thread to suit tap

Handle

6 Place the correct thread in the tap body and tighten it. Press down on the handle and twist. Some people prefer to twist in the same direction and keep turning clockwise, while others prefer to twist backwards and forwards to grind the seat down. It doesn't matter which way you do it as long as you end up with a smooth seat for the washer to sit on.

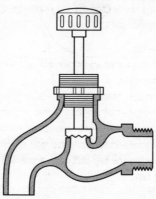

7 When you have finished grinding (you will be able to feel a really smooth seat with your fingers), tip a cup of water down the tap body to rinse away any ground brass which could otherwise get trapped between the seat and the washer.

2.3 Replacing a tap

Changing taps in a bathroom can give a whole new look to the room, and the modern fittings, together with the way they are fitted, bring this job into the DIY zone.

The trickiest part of this job is removing the old taps. Very old taps may be held in with putty or Plumber's Mait (a waterproof plumbing putty), which will bind very hard over time. The back nuts and tap connectors that hold a tap in place and provide the connection for the water are almost impossible to manipulate with anything other than the correct basin spanner which, at the time of writing, costs less than £10 and will save you many hours.

You will need:
* a basin spanner/wrench
* a cloth to clean around tap holes
* the new tap, with all its washers and nuts
* replacement fibre washer if you reuse the existing tap connectors
* a flexible tap connector if your connections do not reach the new taps or are too long.

To replace the tap:
1 First, turn off the water and drain off any water in the pipes by opening the taps.
2 Then undo the tap connector nut which holds the copper pipe onto the thread of the tap. If this is stiff, get someone to hold the tap for you while you apply extra elbow grease. If the entire tap starts to turn, you will again need some help or you can wedge the tap still with a piece of wood pushed between the taps.

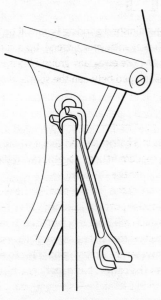

3 Once the tap connector is removed, undo the back nut. This is the nut that actually clamps the tap to the bath and it could be a bit stiff.

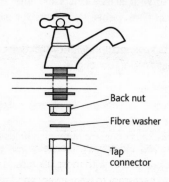

Back nut

Fibre washer

Tap connector

4 Once the taps are off, clean the area round the tap holes. This should be done above and below the bath, basin or sink.

5 Check the instructions that come with the tap to make sure you have all of the required washers, then insert the tap through the hole. When working on a bath it is usually easier to remove the overflow connection from the bath, but remember to put it back!

6 Tighten the back nut of the new tap with all washers and spacers (sometimes called top hats because of their shape).

7 If the existing feed pipes are the right length for the new tap then these can be used; if not, you will need to alter them. If you do reuse the existing tap connectors, replace the fibre washer which you will find in the nut. This washer seals the joint between pipe and tap and without it your connection will leak.

8 If your connections do not reach the new taps or are too long (even a few millimetres can make a watertight joint impossible), the easiest way to connect them is to cut the pipes back from the tap connector and clean the pipe ends thoroughly and then push on a flexible tap connector.

Some flexible tap connectors come with on/off valves attached and these allow you to isolate the water to any tap without turning off the water at the mains.

Push-on fitting
with valve

Tap connector

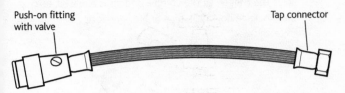

2.4 Unblocking toilets and drains

Unblocking toilets and drains can be relatively easy, but they are dirty jobs. The key here, as with most DIY jobs, is to have the right tools. It is also necessary to wear a very good pair of rubber gloves.

Sinks, baths, basins and shower trays

A sink, bath, basin and shower tray can be unblocked in a few ways.

* An ordinary plunger can be used by placing it over the plughole and pushing up and down on the handle. This creates a force in both directions, compression as you push down and suction as you release. The idea here is that the blockage is dislodged and breaks up, allowing it to flow down the drain.

* Another option is to use what is known as a power plunger. This tool is simply 'pumped up', by pumping the handle at the end, and then placed over the plughole. When you press the trigger, all the compressed air is released, forcing the blockage down the pipe or breaking it up.

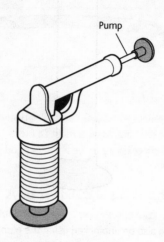

Pump

* A favourite at DIY Doctor is the water injector. Put some water in the sink, basin, bath or shower tray and stand the pump in it. Pull up on the handle to fill the injector with water. Next, place it over the plughole and push down hard, then pull up again. The water is pushed at great force through the blockage and then sucked up again, using the same principles as in the plunger method mentioned above. Repeat this action several times. If your blockage is within a couple of metres of the plughole it will soon clear.
* Finally, for sinks, basins, baths and showers there is the corkscrew cable. The flexible wire is pushed into the drainpipe, wiggled about to break up the blockage, and wound back in – very simple, very effective and available from all DIY stores.

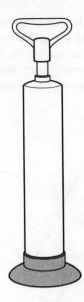

Toilets

A toilet can also be unblocked using the plunger method mentioned earlier if you think your blockage is in the U bend at the back of the toilet. The action is exactly the same, push and pull to break up the blockage.

For blockages that appear to be further down it may be necessary to open the drain manhole to inspect and clear any blockages.

1 First you will need to locate the relevant manhole. You may have a visible soil and vent pipe (SVP) coming out of your bathroom, which you can follow down to the ground and look around for the nearest manhole to it. If it is not the right one, you will need to check further afield.

* There are two types of manhole for the purposes of this project: surface water manholes, which collect water from your rain gutters, and the foul water manholes, which collect the waste water from the sinks, basins, baths, showers and toilets. These will smell, so identification should not be too much of a problem.

* Although your toilet may be blocked, there is a chance that some seepage is occurring through the blockage and you may need to identify this to see which manhole it is running into. This can be done by adding a little dye into the water and watching at the various manholes to trace the flow. Tracing dye can be bought at builders' and plumbers' merchants.

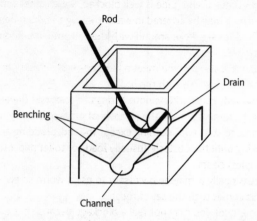

2 Once you have traced the manhole or manholes, you may well be able to rod back up towards the house. The diagram above represents the basics of what you will find in a manhole. Usually a brick-built structure (modern manholes are sometimes formed with pre-cast concrete or plastic rings), with a sloping floor called benching. The benching slopes down into a half-pipe shape called a channel.

3 After carefully removing the manhole cover, which can sometimes be very heavy, the rods should be screwed together one at a time and pushed into the drainpipe. Drain rods come in lengths of 1 metre and are screwed together to make a long length. They are very flexible and are simply inserted into the opening and pushed down the drainpipe.

4 Drain rods screw together in a normal clockwise direction. When you are rodding a drain, the rods will turn in your hand – it's impossible to stop them. In order to prevent the rods from unscrewing, make sure you deliberately turn the rods clockwise as you push and prod. Leaving a length of drain rod in your waste pipe will not help your drainage!

5 Sometimes, if your pipe is well blocked, the channel and benching may be covered in water making the drain hole difficult to see. Poke around with the rod until you find the entrance.

6 You will feel when you meet a blockage and you should then prod the blockage with the rod.

7 Drain rods come with various fittings to screw on the end which, in theory, make the removal of blockages easier. It is best to start with nothing except the rod, prodding and poking until the obstacle (usually loads of toilet paper or nappies) clears.

8 Occasionally it may be necessary to use a worm screw (this comes with the set of rods).

9 Sometimes you may not feel a blockage because it is either too far to reach or too soft to register. At this point, screw on the rubber plunger. Use the rods then as a giant plunger, pushing and pulling up and down the pipe. This will create the same pressures as mentioned above and should release the blockage.

Very occasionally you will meet a blockage which cannot be reached from the toilet end or from the manhole end. This means it may be in the soil and vent pipe itself. Most of these will have access plates, which should be undone very carefully for obvious reasons. A lot of SVPs will be boxed in and this can cause real disruption. If you cannot unblock the drain/pipes by yourself and you feel you have established that the blockage is in your SVP then it may be time to call a plumber. The mess that can be created by this kind of blockage is something you really do not want to deal with if you are not sure of what you are doing.

2.5 Repairing a toilet that won't flush

A toilet that won't flush properly is a frequent problem in homes. If the toilet was working properly and has now stopped flushing, and there is water in the cistern, there are two probable causes:

* the handle is not connected to the flushing mechanism in the cistern
* the flush diaphragm is split.

A cistern allows water in through a valve. There are two main types of valve. The most common is the ball valve; the second, ever more widely used, is the quieter Torbeck valve. Both operate on the same principle: the water inlet is controlled by a valve, which is opened and closed by a lever. The lever, or 'float arm', is raised and lowered by the water in the cistern (this is exactly the same system as that used in cold water tanks in most lofts).

Once the water is in the cistern, a flushing mechanism lets it out again. The most popular flushing mechanism is the toilet siphon. The handle is attached, via a wire, to the top of the flush siphon. When the lever is depressed, or the chain pulled, the flush diaphragm is pulled upwards on the diaphragm frame. Because of the frame underneath the flush diaphragm, the water cannot escape and is drawn up and over into the flush pipe where it runs straight into the toilet bowl.

If the toilet is not flushing properly:

1 Check first that the flushing mechanism is connected together properly. If the lever or chain is not attached to the top of the siphon, it will not pull up the diaphragm and the water will not be released.

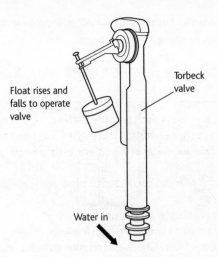

Float rises and falls to operate valve

Torbeck valve

Water in

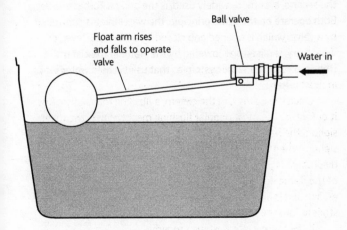

Float arm rises and falls to operate valve

Ball valve

Water in

2 If this is not the problem, move on to check the diaphragm itself. If the flush diaphragm is split, the pressure of the water as the diaphragm is drawn up the chamber simply pushes through the split and does not create any resistance.

The more you flush, the bigger the split becomes. In this case it is time to change the diaphragm.

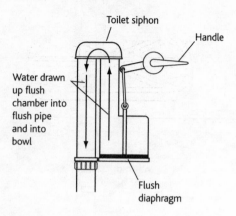

Toilet siphon

Handle

Water drawn up flush chamber into flush pipe and into bowl

Flush diaphragm

You will need:
* a sponge
* a good adjustable spanner or a plumber's wrench
* a replacement diaphragm (available from plumbers' merchants).

To replace a split diaphragm:
1 Turn off the water to the cistern, flush the toilet and soak up any remaining water with a sponge.
2 Once the cistern is empty, unclip the connection between the handle arm and the flush unit.
3 Release the back nut under the cistern and pull the flush unit clear.
4 Unclip the bottom half of the connection clip and pull out the frame, which holds the diaphragm. (There may be a spring over the central dowel – don't forget to return this when reassembling.)
5 Unclip and slide off the diaphragm, replace and reassemble (diaphragm is shown below).

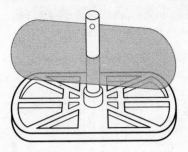

Flush diaphragm

3

other indoor projects

DIY is most commonly associated with projects inside the home from straightforward tasks such as fixing a hook to a wall to more ambitious projects such as plastering a wall. If you want to be proud of what you produce, then buy the right tools for the job and make sure they are the best tools you can afford. Many DIY mistakes, and many poor jobs, are produced as a result of using incorrect tools for the job in hand. When laying any kind of wet covering such as plaster, concrete, adhesive, paint etc., ensure the coverage is even. Plastering is a difficult skill to learn and as with any work or hobby that has a skills element, practice is the key to getting the best possible outcome. It is worth investing say £15 on a sheet of plasterboard and a bag of finish plaster to practise with before tackling the real thing.

With carpentry-related projects, remember: measure twice, cut once. You can always take more off a piece of timber.

3.1 Fixing to masonry

Tools

Fixing brackets for shelves, curtain poles, picture rails, dado rails, anything in the home that requires drilling into masonry or concrete, requires special tools and fixing techniques.

* To get through most masonry surfaces you will need to own or hire a powerful electric drill with a hammer action of no less than 500 W.

* You will also need a masonry drill. You can tell if a drill bit is for drilling masonry or concrete by the shape of the end. A masonry bit has a flat cutting section at the end, which is slightly wider than the shaft of the drill bit. This allows the drill bit to cut its way through the masonry or concrete, and the cut material can escape through the grooves back to the opening of the hole. It is a false economy to buy cheap masonry bits, as they will blunt quickly and, to compensate for this, you will have to push the drill harder, which makes the drill bit wobble and enlarges the hole beyond the size you want. All sorts of complications might then develop which are a major source of questions to DIY Doctor.

* If you need to drill a large hole, say 10 mm, through a very hard surface, it is asking a lot of the drill bit (and drill) to do this in one go, especially if you do not have the powerful tools the professionals use. It is easier to drill a smaller hole first and then increase it with a larger drill bit. You will then end up with a hole the correct size in the exact position you want it.

* When you have drilled the correct size hole you will need to insert a wall plug. Wall plugs essentially come in four sizes and colours. You will see various grey and other

coloured plugs on the market and each has a job to do,
but there are four main types for getting a good fixing to a
brick, block or concrete wall or ceiling:

- yellow plugs fit into holes made by a 5 mm drill bit and
  are for screw sizes 4–8
- red plugs fit into a hole made by a 6 mm drill bit and are
  for screw sizes 6–10
- brown plugs fit into a hole made by a 7 mm drill bit and
  are for screw sizes 10–14
- blue plugs fit into a hole made by a 10 mm drill bit and
  are for screw sizes 14–18.

* Screws come in all shapes and sizes. The larger the number
  of the screw, the larger the diameter. For example, a number
  8 screw is smaller than a number 10. This is the gauge
  number of a screw and is measured using the head of the
  screw rather than the diameter of the shaft. Numbers 8
  and 10 are the most popular screw sizes and suitable for
  most fixings at home.

Tackling the jobs

Now you have all of the equipment you can start
fixing. The two jobs covered in this project are fixing a simple
external candleholder and fixing timber battens to hold basic
shelves.

Fixing a candleholder to an external wall

You will need:

* some tape (e.g. gaffer tape)
* an electric hammer-action drill
* a masonry drill bit of the correct size
* wall plugs of the correct size
* screws of an appropriate size
* your candleholder
* a screwdriver, preferably electric.

To fix the candleholder:
1 First, lay out everything you need.
2 Use a little tape of some kind to wrap round your drill bit
  to mark the depth of the hole you wish to drill. This will be
  determined by the length of the screw you use to attach
  the bracket – in this example the attachment point of the
  candleholder is 7 mm thick and the screw is 50 mm long.

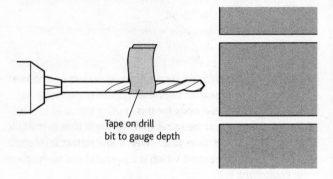

Tape on drill
bit to gauge depth

3 As the screw does not go right to the very end of the
  wall plug, and there is always a little drilling dust left at
  the end of the hole, it is a good idea to add 10 mm to the
  depth of the hole. In this example, 43 mm of screw will be
  in the wall (the other 7 mm will be in the bracket), so adding
  a 10 mm allowance means you need to drill a hole 53 mm
  deep.
4 Next, hold the candleholder up to the wall to mark the
  position of the screws. If this is not possible, measuring
  accurately will do the same job. Mark this with a V shape,
  as shown opposite. The point of the V is where you want to
  drill. Using just a dot or a line can result (after an interruptive
  phone call or a sudden rush to the toilet) in forgetting just
  where the dot is or which end of the line you were going to
  drill to. There is no doubt with a V and most professionals will
  use this method. Make sure that whichever mark you make
  will be covered by the work.

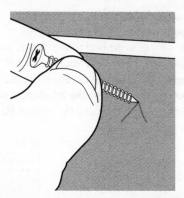

5 Next, drill the hole! Make sure the drill is level and going in at right angles to the wall. Some drills even have tiny spirit levels incorporated into the body for this.

6 Push in the plug you are using, making sure it is all in the hole.

7 Screw your candleholder to the wall. In the picture an electric screwdriver is being used, which is a powerful and useful piece of equipment.

Fixing timber battens to masonry

You will need:

* a pencil
* a spirit level
* some tape (e.g. gaffer tape)
* an electric hammer-action drill
* your timber batten
* a 6 mm masonry drill bit
* wall plugs of the correct size
* screws of an appropriate size
* a screwdriver, preferably electric.

To fix timber battens:

1 Again, lay out everything you need.
2 Hold the batten in position against the wall, making sure it is level.
3 Mark the position of the batten on the wall with a pencil.
4 Take down the batten and drill a 5 mm hole in the centre of it, through which to push the screw.
5 Put the batten back against the wall in line with your pencil mark.
6 Push a screw through the pre-drilled hole and wiggle it on the wall to mark it. Then mark it with a V as shown previously.
7 Use a little tape of some kind to wrap round your drill bit to mark the depth of the hole you wish to drill, as in step 2 of fixing the candleholder.
8 Using a 6 mm masonry bit, drill a hole to the correct depth.
9 Push in the wall plug and screw the timber up tight to the line.
10 You can now use the masonry bit to drill right through the timber and the wall for the other screws. There is no need to keep taking off the batten. Don't forget to alter your depth marker now that you are drilling through the timber as well.
11 Push the wall plug into the timber, turn the screw in a couple of turns and tap it through with a hammer. You will feel the plug slip through the timber into the wall, at which point you screw the screw in.

This method saves you marking each hole individually, which can lead to mistakes. It does eventually blunt the masonry bit slightly, but it takes about 650 holes through timber to do this and the time saved, together with the accuracy involved, makes it worth it.

Battens fixed in this way can be used for shelves and once you have become confident with fixing to masonry you can use exactly the same technique to fix to concrete.

3.2 Plastering

A wall usually requires two coats of plaster: the first coat, or undercoat, is applied to a new (or to be patched) wall; the topcoat, or skim, is applied on top of the undercoat after it has dried. A range of undercoat and topcoat plasters is available; choose the most suitable undercoat for the type of surface you are plastering, and a topcoat that works with the undercoat you've chosen. One-coat plasters are available but the finish is not as good as with two-coat plaster work.

Experiment with different consistencies of plaster by mixing separate piles to see how you like it. With undercoat, you are looking for a muddy consistency – the kind of soft mud you slide through as you walk, but when you pick your feet up there is lots of it stuck to your boots! With topcoat, you are looking for the consistency of thick porridge. Always add the plaster to the water, not the water to the plaster, and mix well to get rid of all the lumps.

You will need:
* a bucket of water
* a large emulsion brush
* a hawk
* a bucket trowel
* a steel trowel/float
* a plastic float
* a small tool for filling narrow gaps.

For undercoat:
* undercoat plaster mix
* a straight-edged length of metal 1.5 m long
* a nail or a small screwdriver to scratch the plaster.

For topcoat:
* top coat plaster mix.

Divide the wall into manageable sections to plaster using 10 mm plaster stop beads (available from builders' merchants). The beads can be fixed to the wall by placing a few small dabs of plaster on the wall and pushing the bead into it. After a few minutes the plaster will grip the bead.

If you have any external corners to negotiate, external 'angle beads' can be fixed in position to make these easier for you. Stop beads can also be bought at 3 mm thick for application and division of the topcoat. Ideally the two coats of plaster should measure 13 mm thick in total, and if the wall is the correct, consistent thickness, the plaster will dry out uniformly, with no cracks.

Laying on undercoat plaster

The application of undercoat plaster to the wall is called 'laying on'. Before you start to apply plaster, damp the wall down with a large emulsion brush and water. Don't let the water run down the wall – use just enough to make it damp.

To apply the undercoat plaster:

1 Place the mixed plaster on your hawk about two trowels full at a time.
2 Then scoop it from the hawk to the steel trowel (sometimes called a steel float) onto the wall. Spread it about so it is slightly proud of the beads on the wall.

Plaster stop beads

3 Then take a straight edge (metal is better than timber) and lay it over the two beads at the bottom of the section you have filled. Push the straight edge against the beads and pull upwards, sliding side-to-side as you go. Do not worry if some chunks come out as you drag upwards.

The gap between the beads is filled with plaster and then the straight edge is pulled up the wall, over the beads, to drag off any surplus plaster

4 Scrape the plaster off the straight edge back into the bucket and go back to your hawk and trowel. Fill the holes and any areas that may be a little low. There should be some surface fissures, but not too many and none too deep.

5 Repeat the process a couple of times until the section is full, flat and relatively smooth, then move to the next section.

6 The metal beads are galvanized (so they don't rust) and will stay in the wall. When you have done two or three sections, the plaster should be beginning to go hard.

7 When you can put your finger lightly on the surface without leaving a mark, it is time to 'rub in'. This means getting the plastic float and rubbing in a circular motion over the wall to close any fissures still remaining.

8 You will feel the surface go smooth under your touch and after a while you should be able to sense any depressions or high spots in the wall. You can add, or remove, a little plaster to correct these.

9 When you have finished you will have a smooth-looking wall.

10 If you have fixed angle beads to any external corners, the undercoat plaster should finish just below the tip of the angle. This will allow you to use the same bead to plaster your topcoat to.

11 After a couple of hours, the undercoat plaster will be hard enough to scratch. Take a nail, or a small screwdriver, and drag it lightly, in a coil shape, over the surface of the plaster. The scratch should be no more than 1 mm deep and all of the wall should be covered, with no more than 150 mm between each of the scratches.

12 Rub over the wall lightly once more with your plastic float, just to flatten out the burrs caused by the scratching.

Your wall is now ready to apply the topcoat.

Applying a plaster topcoat (skimming)

Once you have 'scratched' your undercoat and placed your topcoat beads it is time to apply the topcoat, or skim.

If three or more hours have passed since you finished the undercoat, it's a good idea to dampen the wall again. This will give you a little longer to work with your topcoat (finish).

To apply the topcoat:

1 Position yourself so you can see the thickness of plaster you are applying.

2 Ideally you will apply the plaster in two layers: a very quick 'flash' coat of 1 mm, then a more deliberate coat of 2 mm. Lay it on as you did the undercoat.

3 Try to get the plaster to an approximately even thickness, but do not spend time trying to get it perfectly flat at this stage as this is impossible.

4 Cover the area as quickly as you can, then go back to the starting point and trowel over the plaster again, gradually achieving a flatter and smoother finish.

5 Repeat this as many times as necessary. Each time you revisit it, the plaster will have gone a little harder. It is the timing that is really important in topcoat plastering. Each pass on the hardening plaster should see more and more trowel marks and bumps disappearing.

6 When the plaster is almost fully hard, your final pass will trowel it to a lovely flat finish.

7 To assist with the last couple of passes it is perfectly acceptable to 'flick' water on the wall using the emulsion brush you used to damp the wall down. This will assist in getting rid of trowel marks.

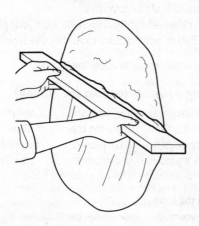

Don't worry if the wall still has one or two marks on it; when it's dry, it can be sanded down lightly.

3.3 Sawing timber

Like all building work, it takes practice and a little know-how to get a straight line when sawing timber.

Look at the teeth on a saw. They are 'set' at an angle to each other. This allows the saw to cut easily through the wood leaving a cut wide enough for the saw to get through without sticking. This only works if the saw is going in a straight line. If the cut you are making veers from the straight in any way, by even a few millimetres, the saw will stick.

The smaller the teeth the saw has, the neater the cut will be. If you are making something which will be seen, a fine-toothed saw will leave you with less sanding to do.

To saw your timber:

1 Make sure you have created a solid platform to work on. If it is possible to clamp the project, even better, but make sure you get some weight on it to stop it moving. It is imperative that the work and workbench are solid and secure. One slight rock and the saw will move off line.

2 Get right over your work. Ideally you should have an eye either side of the saw blade. This should ensure that your cut is at 90 degrees to the timber. If you are over to one side of the work, your saw will be at an angle.

3 Stroke the saw gently; let it do the work. You are only there as a guide.

3.4 Boxing in pipes

The following picture shows a simple pipe boxing. A and B represent, in this case, two walls, with the pipes fixed to or running up wall B. This could just as easily be a box fixed between the wall and the floor if your pipes are running horizontally, with A representing the floor and B the wall or skirting. The principle is the same in both cases.

The materials you will use will vary depending on the size of your box but for most applications either ½-inch plywood or plasterboard is good. Plywood can be bought at DIY stores and in many of them you can (for a small charge) get it cut to size.

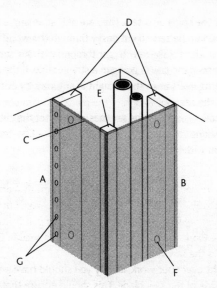

You will need:

* enough ½-inch plywood or plasterboard for your project
* a Jack saw
* three battens (50 mm × 25 mm is usually a good size, although in most applications 38 mm × 19 mm is also fine)
* a tape measure
* a hammer-action power drill
* a 5.5 mm or 6 mm masonry drill bit
* red wall plugs
* 2-inch number 8 screws
* screws or panel pins
* wood glue
* decorator's caulk (flexible filler in a tube, applied using a sealant gun).

(The drill bit, wall plugs and screws listed above are for masonry walls. Different walls will need different types of fixing, so make sure you know which type of wall you have.)

To box your pipes:

1 Fix the two battens (D on the previous diagram) to the surfaces (A and B), as close to the pipes as possible. The screws (F) should be about 400 mm apart.

2 Next, measure the required width of board C.

3 Then measure the length of the piece of board you need from floor to ceiling or whatever two surfaces this box is between.

4 Cut board C.

5 Cut batten E to the same length as your boxing and maybe just a millimetre or so longer. This will give it enough length to fit tightly between the two surfaces and give the boxing greater strength. Be careful not to cut it too long and damage the ceiling or walls as you push it into position.

6 Fix batten E to board C. The batten can be fixed with either screws or panel pins, but whatever you use for any of the surface fixings, remember you may need to decorate, so get the heads of the fixings slightly below the surface of your box. The holes can be filled later. You can use a little wood glue on these joints as well.

7 Having fixed board C to batten E, place them in position against the batten on wall A. A little glue and some panel pins or screws (as shown by G) will hold the board in position, together with the tightness of batten E 'wedged' into position.

8 Now cut the other side of the board and glue, pin or screw into position.

9 Fill all the screw holes and pin holes and then run around the edges with some decorator's caulk to hide the joints between box and walls/ceiling.

10 The box can then be decorated to match the rest of the room.

3.5 Working with skirting, architraves, coving and dado rails

There are many occasions when doing work at home, when angles need to be measured and cut. These angles, when fitting

materials together in two or more sections, are called mitres.
The most common uses of mitres are for putting up coving, cutting
and fixing skirting or architraves, fitting dado and picture rails, stud
walls and roofing. In all cases it is first necessary to establish if your
room is square.

Establishing if your room is square

To use the 3, 4, 5 method (based on Pythagoras' theorem):

1 Measure 3 feet (or metres or any other unit) along
one wall.

2 Measure 4 of the same unit along an adjoining wall.

3 Measure the diagonal line between the two points. If it
measures 5 units then your walls are square. If not, you
will need to mark some points that are square to start
your work.

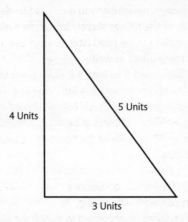

4 Units

5 Units

3 Units

Using mitre joints between skirting boards

DIY Doctor receives hundreds of questions from people about
how they can fill big gaps between skirting boards, caused because
the walls of the room are not exactly at right angles. Rather than
having gaps at skirting joints and having to fill them, it is better to
fit them snugly in the first place, using a mitre joint.

To cut mitre joints in skirting boards:

1 Use the 3, 4, 5 method to check the angle of the walls.
   You can then divide this by two to get the angle at which the
   work needs to be cut. A square 90 degree angle requires
   two separate cuts at 45 degrees.

2 If your wall, doorway or ceiling is not square, you will need to
   buy an angle finder from Screwfix.com to measure the exact
   angle before you can cut the angles or 'mitres'.

3 The following illustration shows the walls along which
   you can imagine placing skirting. On the top example,
   if you had to join the skirting on the indicated line, you
   would need to make two cuts at 90 degrees to get a tidy
   joint. On the middle example make two mitre cuts of
   72.5 degrees each, and on the last example two mitre cuts
   of 45 degrees.

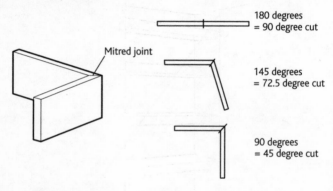

180 degrees
= 90 degree cut

Mitred joint

145 degrees
= 72.5 degree cut

90 degrees
= 45 degree cut

4 The angle should be cut using either a mitre saw or an
   ordinary saw placed in a mitre block. Both are readily available
   from DIY stores.

Using mitre joints in dado rails

The same principle can be applied to a dado rail on the wall
going up a staircase.

1 Draw lines on the wall (using a spirit level as a straight edge)
   at the height you want the dado to go.

2 Where the lines meet at the top of the stairs, measure the angle. An ordinary protractor can be used to do this.

3 Then continue as for skirting boards.

3.6 Making shelves

The project below outlines how to fit shelves into a chimney recess. You can adapt these instructions to suit your own ideas. The principle of fitting shelves can be applied to any type of shelf and, the basics are there for all fitments.

These shelves are called floating shelves as there are no visible means of support. They are very expensive at DIY stores and, in most cases, are a little flimsy. The shelves described below should last a lifetime!

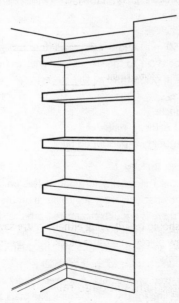

The tops of these shelves were made of redwood (pine), so they could be stained later to match the floor and doors. To hide the support battens the underside is clad with tongue and grooved matchboard. The support battens are 2 inch × 1 inch treated softwood, fixed using red wall plugs and 3-inch number 8 screws.

You will need:

* a pencil
* a spirit level
* some tape (e.g. gaffer tape)
* an electric hammer-action drill
* timber battens
* a 6 mm masonry drill bit
* wall plugs of the correct size
* screws of an appropriate size
* an electric screwdriver
* a Jack saw
* timber cut to the correct size for the tops and fronts of your shelves
* wood adhesive
* 2-inch (50 mm) number 8 screws (four for each shelf)
* matchboard cut to the size of your shelves (readily available in packs from all DIY stores)
* panel pins
* a nail punch
* 50 mm 'lost-head' nails
* some neutral two-part wood filler.

To make your shelves:

1 First, mark out the spacing for your shelves on the wall. Think about what you are going to place on the shelves and make sure there is enough clearance from the shelf above. If the shelves are for books, then be sure to measure the tallest books and designate at least one shelf for them.

2 Attach the first batten to the back wall (see 3.1).

3 With the batten on the back wall fixed solidly in position, mark a level line for the side battens. The mark nearest the front of the batten should also be checked for level from the opposite corner of the batten at the back. If you do not have a spirit level long enough to do this then use a piece of the

shelving timber (after checking that it is straight) on its edge
to sit across the gap, with the spirit level on top.

4 When measuring and fixing the side battens, don't forget
that in this design there is a face timber which is 25 mm thick,
so if you want the shelf to finish flush with the front of an
alcove you must leave the battens 25 mm back from the face.

5 Repeat this process for the rest of the shelf battens.

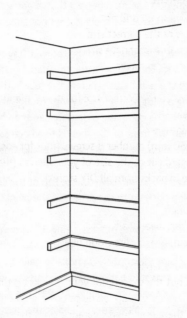

6 The top timbers can now be fixed. Always start multiple
shelving from the top shelf and work downwards. You will not
have any obstructions if you work this way. In this example
the shelf timbers are 150 mm wide and a full width timber
should be used at the front. Any cut timbers should go at the
back where they are less likely to be seen – the chances are
you will need to cut up against the back wall anyway. In an
alcove especially, walls are unlikely to be square.

7 Apply wood adhesive to the top of the battens and then screw the timbers down, with two screws in each end of each timber. Use 2-inch (50 mm) number 8 screws. Countersink the heads of the screws into the shelf.

8 Now fix a centre batten from above, using the same countersinking method. This batten, in this instance, is purely to help support the matchboard that is going to be fixed to the underside of the shelf. It does not support the top planks.

9 The 25 mm 'planks' used for the top will stay rigid to a span of about 1 m. For distances greater than 1 m, fix the centre batten to the rear batten (before the rear batten is fixed) by drilling a pilot hole and screwing through the back of the rear batten. The complete assembly can then be fixed to the wall. When the front of the shelf is fixed across the battens it will give extra support in the centre, allowing a total rigid span of about 1.8 m.

10 Place some wood adhesive on the top of the cross batten and push up to the centre of the planks. Fix from above.

11 Now repeat the same process, using 10 mm matchboard, to the underside of the shelf. Use adhesive and panel pins to secure this timber. Do not use nails on shelves like this as repeated hammering on struts fixed to old masonry can loosen the fixings. As with the planks above, place the full width timbers at the front and cut the final timber to shape at the back of the shelf, against the wall.

12 The last job is to cut the front of the shelves. This is made from the same planks as the top. Carefully measure the width required and cut the timber down. Because of the variation in all timbers it is not safe to assume each front will be the same, so measure each one individually.

13 Once they are cut down, nail each front into the end of the battens. The front of the shelves will be highly visible, so keep the holes as small as possible – 50 mm 'lost-head' nails can be bought for this purpose. These have a small head, which is banged in flush with the top of the timber, then a nail punch is used to bang them in another millimetre or so, allowing them to disappear under the surface of the timber. If done carefully, the timber all but closes up over the head of the nail.

14 Now sand down the edges of the face timbers and any filling. Always use a neutral two-part wood filler for this kind of joinery work. It is more expensive than ordinary filler, but is much stronger and will accept wood stain more easily. It will not stain to exactly the same colour as the rest of the wood as its composition is obviously different, but using a neutral filler will get it as close as possible.

15 Now wax or stain your timber to the required finish and stand back to admire your work.

4

outdoor projects

Many projects outside the home, from paving your driveway to putting up a fence, can be done yourself. The skills needed for the projects in this chapter, such as mixing cement, laying bricks and pointing, are shown in Chapter 5.

It is worth checking with the Planning Department and the Building Control Department of your local council if you need planning permission or approval under the building regulations.

Research and plan your intended project thoroughly. One essential thing to bear in mind is that the ground moves! Do not underestimate the importance of solid foundations and always check levels frequently. It is very difficult to rectify a mistake once things get out of level.

When dealing with mortar, bricks and concrete, wear protective equipment, such as gloves and safety goggles.

4.1 Brick and block paving

Block paving needs to be surrounded by something to give it a firm edge. The edges of any paving are the most vulnerable and you should either lay edging stones or lay an edge of the paving blocks you are using. If using the same paving bricks or blocks to form the edges, they should be laid on a small foundation.

You will need:
* an electric breaker if you need to remove old concrete (available to hire from a tool-hire shop)
* scalping stone (crushed stone aggregate) or hardcore; the former is preferable
* a vibrating plate, which can be hired from a tool-hire shop
* a supply of sharp sand (enough to cover the area to a depth of 50 mm)
* a wooden flooring float or a batten
* paving bricks or blocks
* either a disk cutter (for smaller areas) or a splitter (a proprietary cutter) for a larger area, both of which can be hired from a tool-hire shop
* silver (play pit) sand
* a brush or broom for brushing the sand into the joints.

To lay the paving:
1 Set out the area to be paved and make sure the levels you are laying to will drain water away from the house (note any paving near the house should be at least 150 mm below the damp-proof course).
2 Remove any surplus soil or concrete, which could affect the levels. Concrete can be removed using an electric breaker.
3 Construct a sub-base using scalping stone or very well-compacted hardcore. Scalping stone can be bought from builders' merchants and is ideal for bases of this kind. It is much easier to work with than hardcore and should be laid to a bed of between 100 mm and 150 mm.
4 Compact the scalping stone using a vibrating plate.

5 Then place a layer of sharp sand over the scalpings. This layer should be 50 mm deep.

6 Once the sand is in, compact it using the vibrating plate. Lumps can form in the sand and if these go unnoticed until you compact the pathway, the lumps may burst and a brick or two may immediately drop into the void created.

7 Once compacted, level out the sand using a wooden flooring float or a piece of batten. Make sure you have a completely flat sand base.

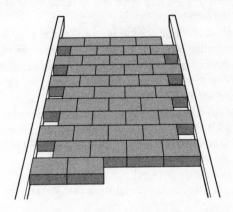

8 Once the sand is laid, the bricks can be laid across it. Make sure you press them up together as closely as possible and bed them down gently in the sand.

9 The bricks should be laid so that the joints overlap, as shown in the illustration above. This will leave gaps at the ends of each row. Bricks can then be cut and placed into the gaps. The best way to make the cuts, if there is only a small number to do, is with a disk cutter. Larger areas require more cuts and it is easier to cut these with a proprietary cutter, or splitter as it is called.

10 Do not attempt to rush this job – each brick has a small spacing burr or two on each side to give a little joint between them, so make sure you lay them square and check if any brick feels like it hasn't gone down properly. On soft sand, it may be that there is a lump of gravel or something in the way, so take the brick out and check. You will be vibrating these bricks down soon so it is important they all sit on the bed properly.

11 When the path is laid and cuts complete, cover it with silver (play pit) sand and brush the sand into all the joints. Again, don't rush this job as it is this sand that binds the paving together and will stop bricks moving once traffic starts to use the path.

12 When you have brushed in as much sand as possible, run the vibrating plate over the path for ten minutes. Make sure you have covered every square inch and do not dwell in one place for too long. Do not clean all surplus sand off the path before vibrating.

13 After ten minutes, tip some more silver sand over the surface and start brushing in again, then vibrate again. Continue with this until you are sure every single joint is full.

4.2 Laying edging stones

A concrete edging stone is a mini kerb. Whereas kerbs are used for roads, edgings are used for driveways and paths. Edging stones come in all shapes and sizes for driveways, paths and garden borders. They are a good way of separating parts of your garden in a permanent way and providing a good solid edge to work to. Some just sit in soil, some on a mortar bed and some need concreting in. The principle is always the same: they are used to stop the base spreading as weight is applied to it and, as such, must be laid in a strong mix of concrete.

Usually, the stone has one rounded 'bull-nosed' edge, which softens the look of the stone and also protects car tyres when used on a driveway. This project deals with straight, concrete edging stones. The illustration below shows edging stones used for a path.

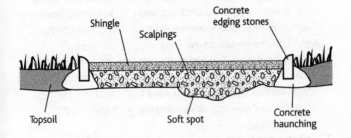

You will need:
* a shovel
* some scalping stone
* some concrete mixed at 6 to 1 (see 5.1)
* a paving mallet or a lump (or club) hammer
* a piece of string slightly longer than the length of the path/drive
* a long piece of timber to level across if using edgings on both sides
* pegs and a spirit level for widths too great to use a piece of timber
* edging stones
* a disk cutter, with stone-cutting disks (these can be hired from a tool-hire shop)
* a wooden or plastic plastering float.

To lay the edging stones:
1 First, excavate the path and dig out any soft spots and spongy areas. Fill these with scalping stone. Once the edgings are down, the finish of the path can be anything you choose – edging stones are ideal for holding in shingle or other loose coverings such as bark.

2 Lay concrete 2–3 inches (50–75 mm) wide and deep along the line you would like the edgings to follow.

3 Lay an edging stone at each end of the concrete line and tap it to level, usually with a paving mallet or the handle of a lump (or club) hammer.

4 Attach a string line to the back edge of the stone, then run it out to the other end of the path and attach it to the edging stone at that end. This second stone will probably be temporary, as it may have to be replaced by a cut stone, depending on the length of the path.

5 Remember to take into account the slope of the path and, if using edgings on both sides, use a long piece of timber to level across. If the distance is too great, transfer the level using pegs banged into the ground and levelling across them with a spirit level.

6 Once the two end stones are in and the string line is in position, lay the rest of the edgings. Tap each one down into the concrete, butting one up against the next one. There is no need for a joint.

7 You may need to cut one or two edgings to fit the length of the path, and this can be done with a disk cutter. Make sure you hire or buy stone-cutting disks, as metal-cutting disks will not cut through stone or concrete.

8 When all the edging stones are in position, place concrete at the back and front of them. The main pressure against the edging stone is almost always from the front, so most of the concrete needs to be at the back as you will probably have a sub-base of some kind at the front.

9 Remember to leave enough depth for a little soil if you are reinstating turf behind the stones, and compact the concrete well using a flat piece of timber or preferably a wooden or plastic plastering float.

10 Angle the concrete away from the stone so water does not sit on top of the concrete.

4.3 Repointing a patio

The ground moves and, in turn, patios move. The first casualty of this movement is usually the cement joints in between the patio or paving slabs.

You will need:
* a hammer
* a bolster chisel
* a plugging chisel
* sand and cement mixture (see 2 and 3 below)
* a brush or broom for brushing the mixture into the joints.

To repoint the patio:

1 If you are working on a patio or paving where little of the existing pointing is left, it is better to cut out all of the old pointing and start again. A hammer and a bolster chisel are the best tools for this, along with a plugging chisel for tight joints.

2 Prepare your sand and cement mixture. The type of sand you use will depend on the width of your joints. For joints that are less than ½ inch (13 mm) you should use silver sand. This is more commonly called play pit sand. Mix the sand with cement at a ratio of 1 to 1 and spread out to dry thoroughly. Do not mix on the patio.

3 If the joints are wider than ½ inch, use sharp sand. Make sure this is dry and that all the lumps are squashed. This should be mixed at 3 parts sand to 1 part cement. This makes it slightly leaner and even more flexible. It should be left to dry as above.

4 Using a bucket, sprinkle the mix along a couple of joints. Then, using a soft brush, brush carefully into the joint. Make sure the joint is absolutely full, even to the point of having to tamp down the mix with a piece of timber.

5 When the joints are full, brush any surplus off the surface and leave. The moisture in the air, plus the moisture from

the ground underneath, will eventually make the jointing hard. This slow hardening process keeps the joint flexible and, providing you have filled the joints up, they will not crack.

Patios can be pointed quite quickly using this method and, providing everything is dry, there need be no staining of the slabs.

4.4 Concreting fence posts

A fence post should be chosen to allow 25 per cent of its length to be in the ground. A 6-foot high fence should have an 8-foot post, with 2 foot in the ground. A 5-foot fence should have a 6-foot 6-inch post with 1 foot 6 inches in the ground, and so on.

For fences of 6 feet and over, 4 × 4 inch posts are recommended; for anything under 6 feet, 3 × 3 inch posts are recommended.

All posts should be pressure treated to avoid rot and wood-boring insects.

You will need:
* the correct number and size of timbers for your fence
* a shovel
* a general concrete mixture (see 5.1)
* a stick or broom handle
* pieces of timber to use as temporary struts to hold the post steady while the concrete dries.

To concrete the posts:
1 Dig a hole three times as wide as the post and as deep as is necessary for the height of the fence. For a 4-inch post the hole should be at least 12 inches wide.
2 Position the post in the hole and then place the concrete mix in the hole, settling it into place by poking it with

a stick or broom handle to make sure no air pockets are present.

3 The top of the concrete should be sloped away from the posts to allow water to run away from the timber.

4 Leave 150 mm between the top of the concrete and the top of the hole for backfilling with soil, and turf if required.

5 Level the post vertically with a spirit level.

6 Add temporary struts to hold it in position for at least four hours to stop any wind or accidental bumping moving it from its vertical position.

4.5 Replacing a damaged brick or ceramic tile

For a variety of reasons, bricks can be damaged, marked or stained. You may simply have had a hanging basket fixed to a brick with a hook in a wall plug and are now left with a messy hole.

You will need:

* a power drill
* a 6 mm or 7 mm masonry bit
* a lump hammer
* a sharp cold chisel
* a jointing or plugging chisel
* a paintbrush or similar
* a little sand and cement mixed to the required strength and colour (see 5.3 and 5.4)
* a pointing trowel.

To replace the brick:

1 First, use the drill and masonry bit to drill holes in the joint surrounding the brick and in the brick itself. The more holes the better.

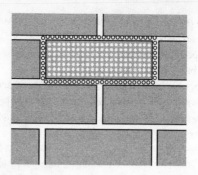

2 Next, using the cold chisel, or even a bolster chisel, chop out the brick. The drilling will have made this considerably easier and if you have drilled all the way into the brick, about 100 mm, you should have no trouble removing all of it.

3 For fiddly corners and sections of the mortar bed, which always seem to want to stay there, use a jointing or plugging chisel. These are really sharp and the acute angle of the blade allows you to get right to where you need to be.

4 Having removed the brick, sweep out the hole with a paintbrush or similar.

5 Place a bed of your sand and cement mix on the floor of the hole and make sure it is a little thicker than the bed joint you removed.

6 Now, if you can, use the pointing trowel to get some of the mixture to stick to either side of the hole. If not, don't worry – it can be forced in later.

7 Now spread some of the mixture on the top of the new brick and pat it down a little to help it adhere to the surface.

8 Push the brick into the opening by sitting it on the pointing trowel and gently lowering it onto the bed of mortar. Some mortar will squash out, so cut this off with the trowel.

9 Wiggle the brick about so it sits level in the opening and the joints line up with the existing joints.

10 Use the pointing trowel to push in more mortar where you can see any voids.

11 Finally, point up the new joints to match the existing shape, using a brick jointer (see 5.5).

This project, although it shows a brick being replaced, can also be used to replace a cracked ceramic tile. When applying the principle to tiles, however, it is important to ensure the drill is not on the hammer setting.

5

basic
building
skills

Both cement and mortar are used in many DIY projects and need to be mixed to different specifications for different purposes. When mixing concrete and mortar it is important to prepare an area which includes facilities for cleaning mixers and tools. Suitable access will also be needed to avoid damage and accidents. Brickwork and blockwork need to be tough.

Bonding, or tying together individual bricks and blocks, can be done in a number of ways. Whichever method is used, it is imperative that the maximum strength possible is obtained for the task of the wall. Practise brick and block laying before you start a project – the wasted sand and cement will be worth it to get a great job on the real thing.

5.1 Mixing concrete

Concrete is a mixture of cement, sand (fine aggregate), small stone or gravel (coarse aggregate) and water. It has many applications, from fence posts to motorway bases and, because of this, there are many different ratios to which the constituents can be mixed.

These instructions concentrate on a general-purpose mix suitable for DIY projects such as garden paths, fence posts and shallow retaining wall foundations. It is a medium-strength mix and is known as a C20 mix. This means it will attain a strength equivalent to withstanding a compression of 20 Newtons per square millimetre after 28 days.

Aggregate

You can buy bags (usually 40 kg) of ready-mixed aggregate. In most areas of the country, this mix of aggregates (sharp grit sand and small stones or gravel) is called 'ballast'; in the West Country it is most often called '½ inch/ 10 mm to dust'. This describes the sieved state of the stone as it comes out of the quarry crushers.

Aggregate can also be bought loose (delivered by lorry). This is generally cheaper and, if you have the room to have it delivered, it makes working a little easier as you do not have to open all the bags.

Cement

Cement can be bought (usually in 25 kg bags, although some stores still sell 50 kg bags) from builders' merchants and, more expensively, from DIY stores. It is crushed limestone, blended with other raw materials (sometimes shale and/or sand), ground into a powder and then heated in a kiln. This process produces a cement clinker, which is mixed with gypsum and ground further to produce the cement.

A cement mixer can be hired from tool-hire shops. If you need to mix a large quantity of cement or your project will last some time (e.g. self-build projects), it might be more cost-effective to buy your own mixer and sell it after completing the project.

Water

Water is a very important part of the mix and the volume
of water used can dictate the strength of the finished mix.
On site, or in ready-mixed concrete yards, a 'slump test' is used
to test the water content of the concrete. A cone made of steel is
used for this test. The cone is 300 mm high, with a top opening of
100 mm diameter and a bottom opening of 200 mm diameter.
The mixed concrete is placed into the cone through the top,
a bar is used to compact the concrete and remove air pockets
within the cone. The cone is then lifted clear. By placing the
metal cone next to the newly formed concrete cone, then laying
the bar on top of the metal cone, it is possible to measure how
far the concrete 'slumps'. A slump of approx 50 mm is acceptable
for C20 concrete.

Quantities

The quantities of aggregate, cement and water you need
will depend on the total amount of concrete you require for your
project, but it is the proportions of the ingredients that is most
important.

The proportions of materials for a C20P (P = Portland cement)
mix are:

1 1 × cement, 2 × fine aggregate (sand) and 4 × coarse
  aggregate
2 if you are using a pre-mixed ballast, then 6 of these are mixed
  with 1 cement
3 in an ideal world, where everything is delivered dry, then
  a water-to-cement ratio of approximately 0.55 should be
  used, e.g. if you require 25 kg of cement in your mix, then
  25 × 0.55 = 13.75 kg (litres) of water. This is the maximum
  amount of water that should be used. Frequently, however,
  the sand etc. is damp, or even wringing wet, and care has to
  be taken to ensure that your mix does not become too sloppy.
  It should be able to support itself, almost fully, in a heap on
  the shovel.

When mixing a very strong mix, normally labelled C35P, the mix is: 1 × cement, 1 × stone and 2 × sand; or 1 × cement to 3 × ready-mixed aggregate.

You will need:
* the correct quantity of ready-mixed aggregate (available from most builders' merchants)
* the correct quantity of cement
* the correct volume of water
* a cement mixer
* a shovel
* a bucket.

To mix the concrete:
1 To ensure a well-mixed batch, add your ingredients to the mixer in the following order: 75 per cent of the water followed by 50 per cent of the aggregates.
2 Add all of the cement and then the rest of the aggregates and the remainder of the water.
3 Don't forget to clean all your tools thoroughly, as it will not take long for the concrete to go hard, making cleaning much more difficult.

5.2 Laying bricks and blocks

It is up to you which bond you choose to build your wall with, but whichever you choose it's a good idea to practise your brickwork before you start a major project.

You will need:
* a wooden batten the length of the proposed height of the wall
* mortar mix (see 5.3)
* a board for placing a couple of shovels-full of mortar on (commonly called a spotboard)
* a trowel
* a spirit level
* a boat level.

What to do:

1 To make sure your wall finishes at the right height, get a
timber batten the same length as the proposed height of
the wall. Using the measurements of the bricks and blocks
you intend to use, mark the proposed courses on to the
batten, working from the bottom up. See where the last
mark comes to on the batten and measure from there to
the end of the batten. Whatever is left over can be 'made up'
by slightly increasing the depth of the mortar in each bed
joint (although these should be no more than 15 mm) or,
if it is easier to add another full course, the bed joints can
be made a little shallower (but ideally no less than 6 mm
deep).

2 To begin laying, place some of your mortar mix on a
spotboard close to the wall. Use your trowel to roll some of
the mortar from the top of the pile downwards until it forms
a sausage at the bottom. Slide the trowel under the sausage
and then let it slide off again into position on the foundation
for the first course of bricks.

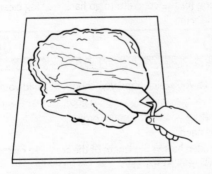

3 Use the point of your trowel to form a V in the mortar bed.
This V allows for displacement of mortar as you push the
brick down. (The same principle can be applied to many jobs,
e.g. ceramic tiling.)

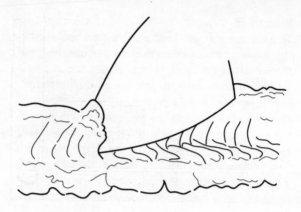

4 Place your bricks carefully but firmly onto the bed. Push down with a slight twisting movement, leaving a bed of 10 mm under the brick. Place the spirit level at the back (or front) of the bricks to check that they are being laid in a straight line.

5 Make sure you fill the joints between the bricks.

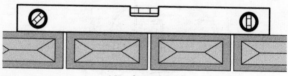

View from above

6 Lay the bricks to stretcher bond (i.e. with their long sides along the face of the wall) and, once you have built two or three courses, put your spirit level on the brick course to check that it is level and then stand it vertically against the ends of the wall to check that it is perfectly upright.

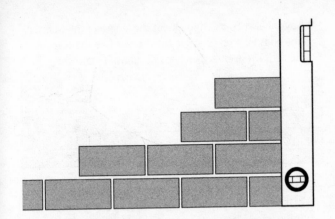

7 Do this for each subsequent course, at the front and at both ends (see the boat level in the illustration below).

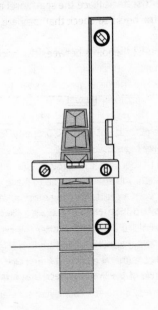

8 Lay the first course throughout the length of the wall, with the ends built up to about five courses (see the diagram below). These ends then become known as corners.

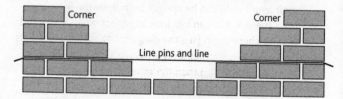

9 When the corners are up, use them as a template for the rest of the wall by stretching a string line between them, using bricklayers' lines and line pins (which can be bought from all DIY stores). Push the pins into the mortar joints and stretch the string between them.

10 Lay the bricks so the top edge of each one is touching the line. If your corners have been built properly, the rest is easy.

Other brick and block laying tips

* If the last brick you have laid is not level, do not bash it with a trowel or hammer, as doing so may knock several others out of position. However robust a brick wall appears to be, while the mortar is wet the bricks or blocks can move all over the place if not handled properly. This is especially true of heavy blocks.

* If your bed of mortar is the correct depth and the mix is pliable enough, you should be able to place the bricks down gently and, with a gentle twisting motion, get them into the correct, level position. Now and again a gentle tap is required with the handle of a trowel but after this tap a bricklayer will always stand back to make sure nothing else has moved. If time and care are taken over the first few courses, the rest become easier. If the first few courses are uneven in any way, it becomes very difficult to achieve a satisfactory finish.

* As you build the wall, check not only the line, level and how upright the wall is, but also check the level across the width of the wall. Bricks and blocks can be level along their length, and can be upright both from the front and from the side, but can still look imperfect when you stand back to check them (see the diagram below). This is always because the wall is not level across its width. The bricks can tilt one way and then the other, but at least one part of the brick is touching the spirit level when it is laid lengthways, so the wall appears to be correct. It takes time and experience to become proficient enough to avoid this problem, but until then using a spirit level, in all directions, is the best way to ensure a good finish to your wall. The result of not doing this may look a little exaggerated in the diagram but, if you try it yourself, you will see it is not!

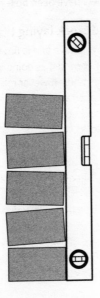

5.3 Mixing sand and cement mortar

You will need:
* sand
* cement and/or lime
* water
* a shovel or trowel for mixing.

To mix the mortar:

1 Place the required quantity of sand in a heap and hollow the heap out a little.
2 Tip in the cement and/or lime required. Mix these together thoroughly.

3 Then hollow the heap out again and add water. If you want to use any additives in your mix, e.g. frost protector, they should be mixed with the water first (read the instructions on the tub).

4 Start putting the mixed sand and cement into the water from around the edges of the heap and mixing from the middle out to the edges.

Quite often you will see professionals mixing mortar in a wheelbarrow. The sides keep the place tidy and stop dirty water running down the drive.

If you have a lot of work to do and are likely to need more than one mix, it is as well to measure your sand and cement accurately. This will enable you to keep the mix to the same consistency and colour throughout the job. Measuring using a bucket helps 'gauge' your mix accurately.

5.4 Matching mortar colours

If you can track down the type of sand used in the mortar you are trying to match, all that remains is to match the cement content. You will need to make up several mixes to get this right.

You will need:

* a small cup or other receptacle
* a way of measuring the sand accurately.

To mix the mortar:

1 Start with a mix of 3 sand to 1 cement.
2 Then move on to 3½ to 1, 4 to 1, 4½ to 1 and so on.
   Do not go past 6 to 1 or the mix will be too weak for ordinary brickwork.
3 Wait until your mini mixes have dried and use the mix closest to the colour of that in your wall.

Some mortars are artificially coloured with a cement dye. This makes the permutations endless. It is important to mix the dye into the cement before you add the water. Dyes are available in a variety of colours from builders' merchants.

Make up a table, similar to the one below to keep track of the proportions of the different experimental mixes.

Mix number	Sand type	Sand amount	Cement amount	Dye added?
1	Soft yellow	3	1	Y
2				
3				
4				
5				

5.5 Pointing and jointing brickwork

Jointing

Pointing and jointing brickwork have these days come to mean the same thing. It used to be, however, that jointing a wall meant applying the desired finish to the joints of the wall as one built it. Pointing was used to describe the operation of filling joints after they had either fallen out or been 'raked' out to change the texture, colour or mix of a bed joint or 'perp' (perpendicular, or vertical joint).

There are four main types of joint, with variations on each one:

1 The bucket-handle joint is so-called because it is the shape of a metal bucket handle. It is formed by running a bricklayer's jointing iron or a length of hosepipe over the joint when it has just started to go hard.

2 The flush or bagged joint is formed by cutting off the mortar flush with the face of the wall. In some cases this is rubbed over with a piece of cement bag or soft brush to close, or fill up, any tiny holes in the surface of the joint.

3 The weather-struck joint can be struck once (a pointing trowel is pushed into the face of the joint at an angle) as shown below. A joint which is struck twice is pointed to the shape of a horizontal V.

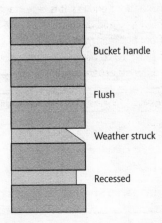

Bucket handle

Flush

Weather struck

Recessed

4 A recessed joint is used when the builder (or architect) particularly wants to show off the shape of the brick being used.

Pointing

Pointing and repointing brickwork and stonework can be very time-consuming jobs and, although they may look easy, it takes experience to get a professional finish. The basic process is outlined here.

You will need:

* a plugging chisel or small bolster chisel
* a screwdriver or similar
* a plasterer's 'hawk'
* a pointing trowel.

To point the brickwork:

1 Cut out all loose and damaged mortar, using a plugging chisel or a small bolster chisel. Rake out very loose mortar with a screwdriver or similar.

2 If you find that some of the faces of the bricks have been damaged as a result of water getting into the joints, you may want to replace them (see 4.5).

3 Mix (and match, if necessary) the mortar (see 5.3 and 5.4).

4 Place a small amount of mortar on a plasterer's 'hawk', as shown below.

5 Push the new mortar into the brickwork joints firmly, using a pointing trowel.